COLLEGE MEMORY BOOK

IT ALL STARTS HERE

BACK TO SCHOOL

GOODBYE SUMMER

10 THINGS I WANT TO SEE, DO AND EXPERIENCE THIS YEAR

1.

....

2.

....

3.

....

4.

....

5.

....

6.

....

7.

....

8.

....

9.

....

10.

....

GOALS & PLANS

- [ ] _____
- [ ] _____
- [ ] _____
- [ ] _____
- [ ] _____
- [ ] _____
- [ ] _____
- [ ] _____
- [ ] _____
- [ ] _____
- [ ] _____
- [ ] _____

DORM LIFE

My Favorites

MIDTERMS

THE GOOD

THE BAD

BIGGEST WIN

■ SUPER EXCITED   ■ SO AWKWARD   ■ THIS WASN'T EASY

NIGHTS OUT

PICS OR IT DIDN'T HAPPEN

current mood

LONG STORY SHORT

LOOKING BACK
REFLECTING ON FALL

HIGHLIGHTS

WHAT I LEARNED

BIGGEST TAKEAWAY

Winter break

NOTES AND PLANS

WAYS I PLAN TO RECHARGE

Who I'll See...

_____

_____

How I'll Relax...

1. _____

2. _____

3. _____

4. _____

GIFT IDEAS:

PERSON: IDEA:

_____   _____

_____   _____

_____   _____

_____   _____

_____   _____

_____   _____

_____   _____

_____   _____

_____   _____

PERSON: IDEA:

NEW
YEAR,
NEW
ME.

GOALS

WHAT ARE **MY GOALS** FOR THIS NEXT YEAR?

WHAT DO I WANT TO **DO MORE** OF IN SCHOOL?

WHAT DO I WANT TO **DO LESS** OF IN SCHOOL?

WHAT IS **THE SCARIEST THING** I WILL TAKE ON THIS YEAR?

MY NEW YEARS RESOLUTIONS:

GOALS & PLANS

- [ ] _____
- [ ] _____
- [ ] _____
- [ ] _____
- [ ] _____
- [ ] _____
- [ ] _____
- [ ] _____
- [ ] _____
- [ ] _____
- [ ] _____
- [ ] _____
- [ ] _____

NEW
FRIENDS

So Much Fun

THE STORY

WHAT I LIKE

■ STELLAR ■ AWKWARD ■ BORING

THE MOST...

■ WORTH IT   ■ HORRIBLE   ■ MESSY

/ /

WORKING HARD.

WHAT I'M LEARNING

What:

Why it's important:

Where I think I'll use it:

What:

Why it's important:

Where I think I'll use it:

What:

Why it's important:

Where I think I'll use it:

What:

Why it's important:

Where I think I'll use it:

What:

Why it's important:

Where I think I'll use it:

What:

Why it's important:

Where I think I'll use it:

What:

Why it's important:

Where I think I'll use it:

What:

Why it's important:

Where I think I'll use it:

What:

Why it's important:

Where I think I'll use it:

What:

Why it's important:

Where I think I'll use it:

SOUNDTRACK
TO MY LIFE

BIG WIN!

☐ **SUPER EXCITED**   ☐ **SO AWKWARD**   ☐ **THIS WASN'T EASY**

current mood

Spring Break

SPRING BREAK PLANS GO HERE

So Much Fun

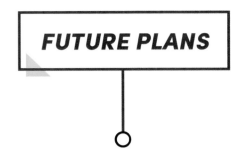

FUTURE PLANS

- [ ] _____
- [ ] _____
- [ ] _____
- [ ] _____
- [ ] _____
- [ ] _____
- [ ] _____
- [ ] _____
- [ ] _____
- [ ] _____
- [ ] _____
- [ ] _____
- [ ] _____
- [ ] _____

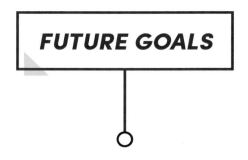

FUTURE GOALS

- [ ] _____
- [ ] _____
- [ ] _____
- [ ] _____
- [ ] _____
- [ ] _____
- [ ] _____
- [ ] _____
- [ ] _____
- [ ] _____
- [ ] _____
- [ ] _____
- [ ] _____

WHAT I'M UP TO

I REALLY REALLY LIKE THIS.

HOW I'M FEELING

_____

_____

_____

_____

_____

FUTURE GOALS

_____

_____

_____

_____

CLUBS

FOR THE RECORD

OFF CAMPUS

HOMETOWN

HIGHSCHOOL FRIENDS

WEEKEND GETAWAY

what's
goin on in
the world

WHERE DO I STAND

My Favorites

BEST FEEDBACK I RECEIVED

1

2

3

4

5

6

7

8

9

10

WHO I'VE MET

CIRCLE
OF
INFLUENCE

Who I can ask to be my mentor?

_____

_____

Who will be at my dinner party?

_____

_____

_____

_____

Who have I met this year?

_____

_____

Most inspiring person I've met.

_____

_____

_____

_____

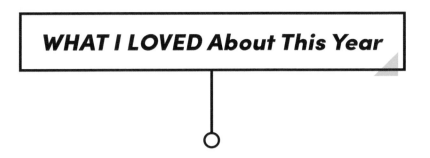

WHAT I LOVED About This Year

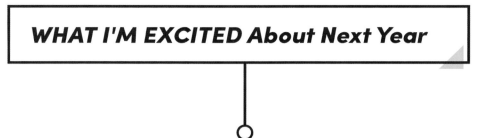

WHAT I'M EXCITED About Next Year

WHAT I'VE ACCOMPLISHED THIS YEAR

1

2

3

4

5

6

7

8

9

10

Published by:
Royal Concepts Inc.
orders@ www.collegememorybook.com

ISBN: 978-1-54397-290-0

Royal Memorabilia is a trademark of Royal Concepts, Inc.

Created for Royal Concepts, Inc.
Creative direction by Seven Almonds

Printed in the United States of America